Picture drawn with thanks

by Jason Parker

The Way Eye See the Game

The Jamie Caven Story

For Dad and Peter

By

Jamie Caven & David Kirby

The Way Eye See the Game

ISBN 978-0-9574988-1-5

Published April 2013

Published by DK DARTS

Printed by Anchorprint Group Limited

Foreword

I first met Jamie Caven in 2006 in Leicester. I remember it clearly as it was the month before I won my 14th PDC World Championship.

It is a well-documented fact that Jamie suffers from diabetes and is blind in his right eye. These facts are never dwelled on and Jamie in no way plays on this element. I can appreciate that it must be difficult to maintain the high levels of concentration required when playing on the professional circuit.

Over the years I have played Jamie many times and always found him to be a worthy opponent. I am confident that we will continue to see Jamie perform at the highest level for many years to come.

Jamie is to me a remarkable sportsman and I feel privileged to have been asked to write a few words at the start of this inspirational book.

Phil Taylor

Sixteen times World Darts Champion

Preface

I had been asked to think about doing a book before, but as I have only been a professional player for 5 years I did not think I had much to write about. I have now chosen this as an opportunity to use it as an inspirational account rather than an autobiography.

Having met Ash Spires and hearing of his turnaround (later in this book), along with the recent passing of two of the largest inspirations in my life, *The Way Eye See the Game* has pretty much written itself.

Jamie

Contents

… I am not really sure if you are standing there, my vision is blurred. Let me go to the toilet first and we can start again. I probably give the impression of being tired but I have just got up; just let me eat. I need to eat the right amount as it is very hard to control my weight nowadays …

My early years

My parents were married in April 1970 here in Leicester and later that year my sister Lisa was born. Lisa is now married with three grown-up children. Three years later in 1973 my elder brother Neil came along. Neil today has already been married twice and has two children.

On a Wednesday in March 1976 I entered the world. To be precise, it was the 10th and I think it was about twenty past six in the morning. The venue for my arrival was the Leicester General Hospital and I weighed in at an impressive six and a half pounds.

Leicester is the second largest city in the Midlands with a population over three hundred thousand. It is a fantastic place to play darts, and many of the pubs still support darts and many teams at all levels.

I am not sure if I have kept that trim over the years, though a great hospital situated on the outskirts of Leicester, in Evington, may have had a lot to do with it.

My mum, Carole wanted to call me Troy, but my dad Neil was not at all happy with this, so they settled on Jamie Robert Caven. I never really asked why Troy, but I bet it was something to do with *Stingray* and Troy Tempest. Mum said she had always loved that name.

There is another excellent Leicestershire darts player: Andy Tempest. You can guess he is nicknamed Troy so it is probably a good job my mum and dad went for Jamie in the end.

My dad was a builder by trade; a ground worker, mainly a drain layer. He had always lived and worked in Leicester. His dad had at one stage moved to Liverpool and that is where I think I get my love for Liverpool FC.

My granddad came back to Leicester when he was about fourteen. I am not sure if granddad had a trade, I cannot remember one. He was certainly not into darts, which started with my dad. I remember he was a big fan of the television series *The Indoor League*.

The Indoor League was a television series filmed in the 1970s. My dad loved it as it featured the current darting stars of the time. It was not just darts as they had loads of other sports: bar billiards, shove-halfpenny, table skittles, pool, table football and arm-wrestling. It was hosted by Fred Trueman wearing a cardigan and smoking a pipe.

Players that featured on this programme included Colin Minton, Tommy O'Regan, Leighton Rees, Conrad Daniels and Tony Brown and of course the programme was produced by a young Sid Waddell. It probably was not as politically correct as required for today's viewers but at least it gave a number of players television coverage during the 1970s.

My mum's dad was originally a cockney and he always kept his cockney accent. He was in the army, I think. He was a hard-working man. He moved to Leicester to help in a factory as a mechanic. This is where he met my nanna who was an overlocker. This was working on machines at high speeds usually hemming large quantities of garments.

I think my mum was also an overlocker in a local factory, but went on to become a shop assistant in our local supermarket. I did have a go once at a family tree but did not get too far. There is a possibility that my great granddad was a vicar.

So far it would seem that my Dad was the only darts player among them all. Although two of my Dad's brothers played. Paul was the eldest and played to a very fair standard. The second brother Bob was a pub player as was my auntie Pauline, who was my Dad's only sister. The third brother John died in his thirties and was the youngest of the three. I believe my mum and dad met in a club.

I consider myself fortunate to have lived at one address throughout my childhood in Leicester. This was not the biggest house and it must have been difficult as the family expanded.

The year of 1976, I am told, was a very hot summer and more importantly John Lowe won the Winmau World Masters, beating Phil Obbard in the final 3-0, which was staged at the Wembley Conference Centre.

You are always hearing how people share birthdays with famous people. Well here is my offering: firstly, Kisaki the Japanese musician; secondly, Haifa Wehbe, a Lebanese singer, model and actress; and lastly Barbara Schett, a tennis player from Austria, who reached number seven in the world rankings. Others of interest are Chuck Norris, Sharon Stone, Prince Edward, Neneh Cherry and Samuel Eto.

My eye situation happened when I was only 15 months old. The story goes that I was out with my uncle when I just started screaming. A sting of some kind was the reason, or so the hospital thought.

Six operations took place, over the next few weeks and there was no hope of saving the sight in my right eye. Although it did not really hinder me as my love for darts came after this incident. I still have check-ups on the good eye twice a year.

I throw my darts with my right hand and it works for me. I have never considered changing this. As you can imagine I do not really see the target and I do not really see the flight of the darts. Over time I have just learned to adapt and trust where they will land.

Even now I probably would not want to change my situation even if an operation was available. Sometimes it seems best to accept the situation you are in and just make the most of it and that is what I do. Obviously there are some practical difficulties to overcome and I am very lucky that my family and friends help me with driving as insurance, for instance, is prohibitive.

I know there has been a lot written about my eyesight but it is not something I intentionally talk about. I am not looking for sympathy or compassion; I just want to get on with the job of playing professional darts. From as far back as I can remember I have loved the sport. It was my only passion from being a toddler and I got my inspiration from my dad, who used to be a decent pub player.

My dad also played a bit of Superleague and was a house champion for the News of The World in the 1970s and 1980s. This contest was England's first national darts competition from the 1940s through to 1990. In the year I was born 1975–76, Bill Lennard beat Leighton Rees 2-0. The game was from 8 feet, which must have been interesting, especially switching back to 7 feet 6 inches or the current standard distance of 7 feet 9¼ inches. The News of the World Tournament was played again in 1997 – won by Phil Taylor beating Ian White in the final.

My dad also played at The Tiger public house in Leicester. The pub was demolished during the 1980s and became a housing estate, as the grounds it stood on were so vast. It was certainly a pub with character and it is a shame it has gone.

I am not a darts historian, but I think Superleague darts came about to allow local leagues to put forward their best players to compete in a separate competition. It must have been quite an honour in the early days to be picked for your local Superleague teams. That is not to say it has diminished in standing today but I think it is just different. A lot of county set-ups use these superleagues to select their county squads. I think though it does give a natural league pyramid progression, which is easy for players to follow.

My favourite player always used to be Eric Bristow. At that time his main rivals were John Lowe and Jocky Wilson. There were the likes of Big Cliff, Bob Anderson and Keith Deller, to name but a few, but it always used to be Eric who I would shout for. It would seem, even now, that Eric was instrumental in promoting darts, especially in the 1980s. Eric brought something to the game that allowed the sport to gain a worldwide audience. I loved watching him play, particularly when representing his country.

I vaguely remember being pushed in my pushchair at a fairground and screaming at a darts stall until I was allowed to have a go. I had to stand on the barrier of the stall and throw my darts, although they probably hit the board or the wall it was attached to! I know it sounds ridiculous but I can actually recall this. I do not think I pierced any goldfish bags. I am even not sure if we paid for my go.

Me and my brother Neil

I started school at Southfields Nursery in 1979. Then attended Southfields Infants 1980–83 and Newry Junior 1984–87, although I attended my dad's old school, Linwood Boys, in 1984 as Newry was being refurbished. This was followed by Mary Linwood School from 1987 to 1992. My last school closed in 1997 and became an annex of the Riverside Business and Enterprise Centre, now part of the Samworth Academy.

I enjoyed English and maths and later cooking and graphic design and art. I was never one for science and struggled with PE as I was a bit of a chunky kid. I still enjoy cooking and will often be found in the kitchen at home.

Those who have been to my house will probably have sampled Debbie's cooking; she is good and a fully trained chef. Anyway just ask next time and leave it to me to cook.

As I grew up the bedroom door was the home of the dartboard. The outside of it, which led to the upstairs landing, was perfect for it, and this became a monument of history as the board was moved up the door as the years passed and as I grew. The holes surrounding where the board used to be could be seen as the board was moved up.

My brother played darts with me as a youngster. He won once or twice, but nine times out of ten, I would give him a bit of a pummelling. This has not stopped him continuing to follow me throughout my career. Lisa, my sister, is pretty keen too as are my nieces and nephews.

It has been difficult for Neil to come to the big tournaments as he is in a wheelchair. He suffers from an adult form of Adrenoleukodystrophy (ALD). This is an inherited disorder and affects his muscle coordination. For a long time my brother walked with a limp and it just became worse and worse. He will now always be in a wheelchair.

ALD is a rare disorder inherited on the X chromosome leading to progressive brain damage and failure of the adrenal gland. Adult onset ALD usually starts between the ages of 20 and 35 with stiff, weak and paralysed limbs.

The X chromosome is one of the two chromosomes that determine the sex of numerous animal types, and the other is the Y chromosome. The X chromosome was named for its exclusive properties by early academics and this gave rise to the naming of its matching Y chromosome as this was the next letter in the alphabet.

His present wife Tania now cares for him.

Sadly my cousin's son Callum died from the children's form of this disease in 2011. Callum 'Smiler' Smith was so nicknamed due to him always laughing and smiling.

This disorder is passed on through the female genes and I think it misses every other generation. I have been tested for it.

I try to see Neil each week and he is upbeat about his situation, which I think is very uplifting. Tania and Neil have now been married for nearly 6 years and have five children between them. I am not sure why they do not have any children of their own as I am sure there is no physical reason why they could not.

I have now become used to seeing Neil in the wheelchair. I am not sure he will ever work again, but he has had a lot of jobs. He worked in a slaughterhouse and as an apprentice on a building site, amongst others. It is very difficult being on disability benefits but he gets by. Tania adores Neil and does so much for him and really does not show any stress from it.

Neil's children, Allyssa and James, from his first marriage now live with their mother in Canada. I should really visit, but in previous tournaments out there, time and distance have been a factor. I plan this year to get over and see them. Facebook comes to the rescue and when I get the hang of Skype I might have a go with that. They always ask how the darts are going but I am not sure how much they actually follow darts or me.

Lisa takes after my mum and dad in that she has been happily married to the same person and has three lovely children.

It is somewhat ironic that Neil is the only one in our family with a current driver's licence. My mum and dad have never driven and we were always lucky to have friends that would give us a lift when needed. Fortunately I have never had an interest in cars.

Overall it was a good time. My mum and dad always worked hard and with school and work being local, childhood was a happy time especially for me.

The picture below is one I created to celebrate the 40th anniversary of the United Nations Universal Declaration of Human Rights. I received a certificate from Leicester United Nations and Amnesty International thanking me for my contribution.

My picture to celebrate the 40th anniversary of the United Nations Universal Declaration of Human Rights.

With graphic design I enjoyed the challenge of reproducing the intricate three-dimensional drawings we were given. I still enjoy drawing and probably should make more time for it. I have drawn a few bits but I am not sure where they are. I drew a picture of George Michael the singer, and in my opinion it was brilliant.

Love of Liverpool FC and drawing

In science we always seemed to be cutting something open, which was gross. I was a bit squeamish back then. I was constantly happy to find a partner who would do the dissection whilst I dealt with the notes and recordings.

Looking at me now you would not believe that I was chunky at school. I always played football at break and lunchtimes.

I played in a charity match in 2012 and was captain. If you noticed I had to play on the right side of the pitch. This was because of the blindness in my right eye. This way I could always see to my left and the field of play.

Another one of my pictures

I recall I was sent to the head teacher's office a couple of times for being cheeky, but to be fair I was no worse than any other kid at the time. I had a letter sent home once for gambling. A group of us would use our dinner money to play the game 'nearest the wall'. You would stand at a line and toss either a 10p or 20p coin towards a wall and the nearest collected the pot. I was only in my second year at senior school so aged only 12 or 13 and when caught we all had a letter to take home to our parents explaining the act. Mine stayed on top of my wardrobe for around 8 months before being destroyed. My parents never got to see the letter.

As to my heart, there was not any particular girl that was my childhood sweetheart, although I do remember my first as an infant, Reagan Oates, and before that there was our neighbour's granddaughter, Nicola, who used to come round for a game of hide and seek. I think I still have a picture of the pair of us. These were the only two that I remember during my school days.

I cannot remember any further loves; I never went out on a date. There may have been one or two at the school discos but none that stick in my memory.

Whilst at school I was a football fan, as most kids were. I supported Liverpool FC and that continues today. I go to as many games as possible, though as we compete mainly at weekends it does not give me much chance. I was also a big darts fan in my schooldays, but I did not talk much about darts at school as not many were avid followers like me.

I do not think teachers had much influence over me, as all I remember was thinking you cannot talk to me about darts so I am not really interested.

My first trophy, runner-up at the Beesons, Torquay aged 11

The eye did not affect school really as I was used to it. Just like everyday life really because it happened when I was a toddler.

On the 20th March 1992 I produced my Personal Statement for my National Record of Achievement. This is a copy of the text:

"My name is Jamie Caven and I am 16 years old. I have been at Mary Linwood for 5 years. My first year was very easy, but it was harder as the years passed. When I reached the fourth year I realised I needed to work harder, because most of the work was going to be entered for GCSE.

"My attendance has been fairly good and when I leave school I want to work anywhere that is involved in retail. When I went on Project Trident I worked at Burtons. I did not know what I wanted to do when I left school, until I went there. The staff were good to get on with and the hours were good, so any job like that would suit me.

"I have been on several trips with the school. I have been to France twice and I have been to the American Adventure four times.

"My hobbies include darts, snooker, pool and football. I also enjoy swimming."

In the build-up to leaving school we were made aware of college and university, but to be honest, I only had one interest and that was the dream of becoming a pro dart player.

I left school in June 1992 after completing my GCSEs. The results were average. I had no idea how I was going to make a career in darts work, I just knew that my heroes were playing darts and that is what I wanted to do. The likes of Bristow, John Lowe, Jocky, Cliff Lazerenko and Bob Anderson, who was just coming on to the scene, oh and Dennis Priestley.

All I wanted to do at that time was play on the Lakeside stage, but in the end I never achieved this ambition of playing on that stage. Who knows, there may be a competition in the future where I can achieve this milestone?

The Embassy World Championship was started in the early 1970s after the British Darts Organisation (BDO), which was founded in 1973. Since 1986 the BDO has been holding their World Professional Championships there. I think the first winner was Leighton Rees in 1978 and after moving to the Lakeside the winner in 1986 was Eric Bristow, beating Dave Whitcombe in the final 6-0. Not a bad average either for Eric with a 94.47.

When Phil Taylor beat Mike Gregory in 1992 he had a 97.59 dart average. Eric also had two 97.50 averages in 1984 and 1985 in the finals. These are not a bad set of averages even in today's modern game.

I was already in regular teams and had almost 3 years' experience. I wanted to get a job and any job as soon as possible to enable me to earn money to pay for my league fees and to have a few quid to play on a Monday and Tuesday.

Winning the Coronation Cup in the Everards Darts League in 1992

The start of my darting life

I played my first league match when I was 13 for Eyres Monsell WMC, which is a great club not far from where I used to live. (I still go back and we have some great exhibition nights there.) It was the end of the season on a Friday night, in the Leicester Trades Darts League and the team were a man short.

This league is now the Leicester Friday Darts League but was formally known as the Leicester Trades Darts League. The league was established shortly after the Second World War and was called the Leicester Trades Darts and Snooker League. The snooker fixtures were discontinued in 1960 due to the lack of support. The league carried on as the Leicester Trades Darts until 1998.

The match could no way dictate anything regarding the way the league would finish but we played Marlow & Lunn and I remember it so well, as the opposition laughed at our captain, Dave Glover, when he explained that we were a man short. Although we lost 4-1, I averaged almost 85 and had plenty of offers to play for other teams the following season, including the Post Office side, who won the honours almost every season with their squad full of Superleague and county players.

During these early days I remember that most of my friends were more than twice my age. Dave Hayes was a father figure to me as he used to be in the same team as my Dad. Owen Worth was a very good friend of mine, sort of a best friend although he is almost 10 years older. Dave Parkinson, Nick Langton and Steve Neal were all good pals and we played in the same team several times each week in different leagues.

During my teenage years there were many memorable games I can recall. I played Martin Adams at Southport Pontins in the first round of the singles as this was the venue for the inter-county knock-out cup. Obviously Adams was a Cambridgeshire representative and I was on behalf of Leicestershire. I beat him 3-1, but complacency got the better of me and I was beaten a couple of rounds later.

I also played Ronnie Baxter at the Welsh Open in the board final and went down 0-3 to the Rocket. He was a BDO star in those days.

I did not play the likes of Taylor and Bristow in the early PDC days, as their events were a closed shop. Although I did play Eric in April 2000 in a head to head, which I won 13-4.

I played top player Kevin Kenny from Merseyside in a county match – it was the game after I hit the top average of the BICC of 37.58, against Reg Brobson of Lincolnshire. It was my second ever A game – I won in darts of 14, 14 and 12 in a 3-0 win. I won £200 from the BDO for this achievement.

Against Kevin, I lost 2-3 but this was a day after I had returned from a 2-week family holiday in Alcudia, Majorca. I took my darts but there was no dartboard in sight! When I returned home, we landed at East Midlands airport and I caught the train to Liverpool and stayed with my Uncle Ray. He wears his heart on his sleeve and gets very excited – he claims to be one of my biggest fans and calls me 'Hero' on Facebook or whenever we talk.

Uncle Ray is the brother of my mum. My other uncle, Melvin, asks how it is going whenever I see him. Aunty Pat, mum's sister does too, but her husband my Uncle Steve has a great passion for darts and calls me regularly.

My first job was for a stationery firm called Stat-Plus Ltd. I saw this advertised in the local paper. I worked in a warehouse dealing with solicitors and accountants on an account basis. I did general warehouse duties – picking and packing orders of stock, law forms and letterheads. It paid about £4k a year; this was enough to pay for my darts. It was my mum who encouraged me to get a job. Until then I just borrowed a few quid from my dad to play darts.

I started work there on 18th January 1993; I know it was that date as it was my dad's birthday on the 16th, which was the Saturday and I started on the Monday. I stayed there for almost 2 years. I was offered a placement at Barratts Shoes in Leicester City Centre, but it was a Youth Training placement which only paid £35 per week whilst training.

I opted for Stat-Plus the £80 per week position as it was closer to home and gave me twice as much money for darts.

The first song that was on the radio when I walked through the door was 'Ordinary World' by Duran Duran. This was the first single on their 1993 album *The Wedding Album*. This song was further immortalised when Simon Le Bon sang with Luciano Pavarotti to help children who suffered during the conflict in Bosnia and Herzegovina.

I played county youth a year or two after I started at senior level. This is because in the early 1990s county youth was not played as a team format, or at least certainly not by many counties. If it was, it would have only been where there was an abundance of talent at the time, in counties such as Essex, Hampshire and London.

However, although we did not have regular fixtures in the BICC youth, we did have a team as did many counties in the BICC Youth KO cup, which was played after the British Teenage Championships and was held at Granby Halls in Leicester.

34

Granby Halls is no longer there. It was knocked do
around a decade ago and is now a car park situated next
to Leicester Tigers RFC. The Halls was a great place for
live music, sports and exhibitions. I even went roller
skating there. It always seems a shame when places like
this go because it has specific history. It was initially
built as an army training facility for troops in the First
World War.

With the Tigers expanding their stadium to where
Granby Halls used to be, it is not too bad as they are a
pretty decent rugby side.

My first County shirt taken on my debut at 15 in the game versus Durham

In the BICC Youth KO cup we finished second and third in consecutive years, to Essex and Hampshire respectively.

Perhaps this spring-boarded us into becoming a team in the BICC Youth Championships a couple of years later. Because of the age restriction when I joined the team in 1995, I only had a couple of seasons left until I reached 21.

I qualified for the British Teenage Singles Championships three times but my best result is joint 9th. This is an annual open tournament run by the BDO. My final appearance in the event was as current World Youth Champion and I was possibly the favourite for the event, but it was a tournament that never seemed to work for me.

I never played International Youth or Senior County level, as the internationals at youth level were not into playing when I played youth and I think I just was not consistent enough as a county player.

I remember, at the age of 11, in 1987 playing at a holiday caravan park called Beesons in Torquay. It was a junior event at which you had to be at least 13. I was there with my brother and our parents as my dad had won a darts event at the holiday park we used to go to on the Isle of Wight.

Normally my sister would be there too, but for some reason she did not come to Torquay. Mind you she would have been around 17 so she would not have been interested. We used the holiday park on the Isle of Wight called Fort Warden for around five consecutive years. I believe now it is a housing estate, which is a shame as I am sure I would have returned there before now as I have many fond memories of the place.

Only one of them was for a youth darts event as I was only old enough on our last visit – I remember winning the event with ease nevertheless.

My second win came a year later at Presthaven Sands in Prestatyn, Wales, with my grandparents. I remember being the only person on the dartboard the night before the event, as all the other kids were watching England with their parents lose on penalties to Germany at Italia '90 in the semi-final.

I recall holiday romances with the Isle of Wight holiday a girl called Tina from Tamworth aged 13 as I was and the year later in Prestatyn a girl called Karen from Stoke aged 16 as I was 14. These both ended after the holidays.

At the winners event my dad had qualified for at Beesons I recall my dad being a beaten quarter-finalist, and I had a throw with the other kids before their competition began. My dad sneakily entered me. As I say, I was only 11 but I was not quizzed over this as I probably just looked a little smaller than the other kids, but was certainly as good as any of them there. I lost in the final, and although I should have been satisfied with doing well, I was very disappointed.

My first Superleague season in 1991 was fairly successful as far as I can remember. I was 15 and played around 14 out of 18 games. I finished in the top 20 of the averages and made my debut for Leicestershire 'B' towards the end of the season. I think it was against Durham, but was not very good; I lost 0-3 and was as nervous as can be. I rectified that though, as I won my next match fairly comfortably.

I had my first man of the match the following season with a 26.84 average. The final game of the season, I was put into the 'A' team for the first time. We had already won promotion and on the weekend we registered a 31-5 victory against Clwyd and fortunately enough this included my debut win in the 'A' team.

The following season being my second ever 'A' match was at home versus Lincolnshire, where I registered a 37.58 average and I think that is the highest ever for a Leicestershire player (112.74) – this included five missed doubles, all at the tender age of 17.

As far as I can remember I left school without a girlfriend as I had too much interest in darts to be interested in girls.

I did though have a passion for music. In the early 1990s I was into Nirvana, whose album *Nevermind*, rocketed up the charts in the year I left school. The Cardigans formed in 1992 as did China Black, who had a massive hit with 'Searching'.

I used to like Shakespears Sister, Right Said Fred (as I look a bit like them hairstyle-wise!) 2 Unlimited and Ocean Colour Scene. I liked a variety back in the day.

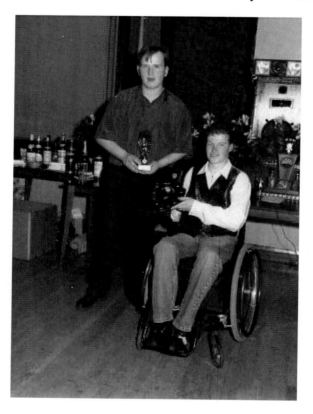

Me and Paul Gibson

Paul is brother of Adam Gibson another good youth player. Paul was a very good youth player who pushed Colin Lloyd close in a youth event (British Teenage) at Granby Halls, Leicester. Paul came off a high speed motorbike, which left him paralysed.

The Winmau World Youth Masters 1993

I entered the World Youth through the Leicestershire system. I had to play the other kids from the county and at the time there was no youth side, although I had quite an advantage being recently selected as a county A player and having a couple of years' experience at county level.

After winning the Leicestershire region, I had to play a Midlands final where all the winners from the Midlands counties played off for one spot at the finals as one of England's eight representatives.

I won the Midlands region, beating Darren Wren in the final. Darren was Worcestershire's qualifier and also played county darts, but for the Worcestershire men's B.

I think Worcestershire were a division higher than Leicestershire at the time and I knew him well as he beat me in the final of the Midlands qualifier the previous year and was a beaten semi-finalist in the 1992 world finals. In fact this was a recent note from Darren:

"It has been 20 years so any details I have about the matches themselves I have forgotten about, what I do know is that both games in 1992 and 1993 were very close, I beat Jamie to qualify for the Winmau World Youth in 1992 and I reached the semi-finals, the following year 1993 Jamie beat me to qualify and went on to win it. I don't know whether Jamie remembers what the games were like or if anything had been officially recorded. As for me personally: - D.O.B

19/04/1976 I'm married with one daughter and one more on the way. Living in Kingswinford in the West Midlands."

Scott Rand from Coventry, who is also a full-time pro in the PDC, was Warwickshire's representative that day. Scott is a year older than me and also lives in the Midlands. Scott joined the PDC in 2009/10 and I now play alongside him on the professional circuit. As we are fairly local we also run into each other quite a bit in neighbouring competitions.

The day before I went to London for the finals I had to let my employers at Stat-Plus know I had to have the Friday off. I do not know what possessed me to not tell them I needed it off before, but maybe I was worried in case they did not authorise it. I nearly lost my job as I told them at the last minute!

I travelled down to Earls Court with my dad for the world finals and remember some comments from some of the other finalists about me hitting a 37.58 per dart average in the Inter-Counties Championships a couple of months earlier.

We arrived on the Thursday evening and I bumped into Kevin Kenny from Merseyside who was ranked around six in the world at the time. He was a little intoxicated and reminded me of our recent county match.

After watching a couple of the final qualifying rounds being played for places in the upcoming Embassy World Championship (Lakeside), I went to bed to get plenty of rest.

The Friday morning all competitors were there warming up and included Michael Barnard who was at that time like the Phil Taylor of the youth game. Michael plays on the Pro Tour today and we sometimes reminisce about the youth days.

World Youth semi-final versus Michael Barnard

He won the world youth in 1991 along with every other youth title. There were world qualifiers from Canada, America and Brazil etc. along with the other home qualifiers from the holiday parks around the coast of the UK.

My first match was against a Brazilian champion called Samantha Dart! What an omen of a name and all I was thinking was do not lose to a girl! I beat her 3-0, then Canada's Chris Greenwood soon followed by the same score. After beating Samantha Dart I remember hitting a 147 check out and Stacy Bromberg then telling me she thought I would win it.

A couple of matches later I had reached the quarters. So my final match of the day, where I lost my first leg of the tournament was against Michael McLoughlan from Tyne and Wear. After winning 3-1 I was told I was through to the semi-finals.

I was ecstatic. I was due to play Michael Barnard first game on the Saturday. I did not sleep much that night, but was ready to play on the Saturday afternoon after the men's and ladies matches had got down to the semis.

I beat Michael Barnard 3-2 and awaited the winner of Merseyside's Lee Palfreyman (who had travelled with Kevin Kenny and was much fancied by him to win it), or Italian, Christian Scribetta. Lee still plays on the PDC circuit. Lee came through so it was him who stood in my way. Christian has played the odd Euro event since then.

I remember the final being a very nervy affair but I came out on top 3-1 and was met at the bottom of the steps by my proud dad and an explosion of applause from the crowd.

Steve Beaton was the men's Masters' Champion, and Mandy Solomons won the ladies. Steve is still going strong and what longevity as he turned professional back in 1993. He is known as the Bronzed Adonis and always seems to feature in the top 32 in the PDC.

Mandy was certainly an exceptional player of her time and was around with the likes of Linda Batten, Sharon Colclough and Maureen Flowers. I believe Mandy has since retired from darts.

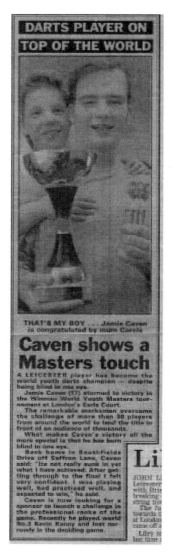

DARTS PLAYER ON TOP OF THE WORLD

THAT'S MY BOY . . . Jamie Caven is congratulated by mum Carole

Caven shows a Masters touch

A LEICESTER player has become the world youth darts champion — despite being blind in one eye.

Jamie Caven (17) stormed to victory in the Winmau World Youth Masters tournament at London's Earls Court.

The remarkable marksman overcame the challenge of more than 50 players from around the world to land the title in front of an audience of thousands.

What makes Caven's victory all the more special is that he has been blind in one eye.

Back home in Southfields Drive off Saffron Lane, Caven said: "Its not really sunk in yet what I have achieved. After getting through to the final I felt very confident. I was playing well, had practised well, and expected to win," he said.

Caven is now looking for a sponsor so launch a challenge in the professional ranks of the game. Recently he played world No.3 Kevin Kenny and lost narrowly in the deciding game.

Me winning The Winmau World Youth Masters 1993 and thank you to the Leicester Mercury

48

The next couple of weeks were crazy with East Midlands Today doing a feature on their news programme and lots of radio and other media stuff happening. This was my dad's proudest moment and one I will never forget.

When I became World Youth Champion, Stat-Plus were then interested in sponsoring me. But as a cocky 17 year old I told them to up my wages significantly as they only wanted me as a world champion, which would generate more business and in turn, make me work harder for them. We decided it was best not to take the sponsorship, as they basically wanted free advertising in any case.

Trophies at Mum and Dad's house

Shortly after winning the World Youth Championship at the end of 1993, I travelled to Eastbourne with Ricky Sudale and his dad. Ricky was one of the top players around Leicester during my county days. In all fairness he was the top player. We were going down to the south coast to play in the weekend festival and me and Ricky were going to play together in the pairs. We travelled down to The Ridings Hotel on the Friday morning, which was run by a Chinese family. The bonus of staying there was a 15 per cent discount at the family restaurant!

On the Friday I was picked up from The Ship Inn on Soar Lane, Leicester. The Ship was one of the top darts pubs in Leicester during my teens, and it regularly held knockouts on Friday nights for a cash prize. At Eastbourne there was a mixed pairs on the Friday evening, and I paired with Nadine Bentley from Cambridgeshire who was to later become a county team mate at Cambridgeshire.

We were beaten in the quarter-finals by Ronnie Baxter and Sue Talbot, who was a very good player. She was a Suffolk County and England International. Although we had a good run we won no prize money. There was the singles and pairs to go over the weekend. I never arrived at any of the events as I woke up in hospital on the Saturday afternoon. I vaguely remember going to bed very tired and as I could not be woken in the morning, Ricky told the owner to open my door or he would knock it down!

They agreed to open the door and I was found in a heap on the floor. I went to Eastbourne hospital and stayed on the Berwick ward for 5 days before I was picked up by my parents. Ricky reminded me for quite a while after about the weekend he saved my life, and I think there is a certain amount of truth in that.

Sophie and Molly

I met Mel when I was 18 in 1994 and she was my first real girlfriend. Her whole family are in to darts and have been involved at county level for quite a few years. Mel is the mum to both Sophie and Molly.

We lived together in a council house in Leicester. I managed to get a job at Bradgate Bakeries, a Leicester based company, that opened in 1993. This was a shift arrangement from 2 until 10 pm Sunday to Thursday. This gave me the opportunity to still play some darts but not nearly enough. It was more important at this point to get more income and that is why I had already left Stat-Plus.

The darts had to take second place as we needed the money because we were about to start a family. Sophie was born a few months after starting at Bradgate Bakeries and Molly was born a little more than two years after Sophie.

This was a good period of my life and it seemed that perhaps this was a recipe for a lasting relationship, just like my parents. This was my first love and I had two beautiful girls.

During this period I underwent surgery twice and Mel stood by me, along with my family. I am really not sure why these things happen, but after 4 years we both felt we wanted to split. There was no obvious reason. Neither of us had found anyone else. It was just one of those things I suppose. We were both very young I guess.

I still see the girls regularly. Sophie plays darts for the county youth team in Leicestershire. This is run by Alan White and they play from the Enderby and District Social Club. A 13.89 is Sophie's highest recent average at County.

1996 and diabetes

Three years after winning the World Youth Championships I started to suffer from a series of blackouts and was given medication for epilepsy. The doctors could not understand why the medication was not working because the fits continued with the medication.

Epilepsy affects the brain and causes seizures or 'fits', the most common symptom. This is because the cells in the brain communicate with electrical impulses. During an epileptic fit these impulses are disrupted causing the brain and the body to behave abnormally with loss of consciousness or convulsions.

Over a period of 6 weeks these intensified until a day in July I collapsed at my home in Leicester.

The next thing I recall is waking up in an ambulance. I was taken into hospital after having a nasty seizure one morning and as tests were done they realised that my blood sugar levels were low; like a diabetic's would be. I had a series of tests including an ultrasound scan, where they noticed something that looked like a mole on my pancreas.

On 25th July 1996, surgery was performed as an exploratory operation, as the doctors were not sure what they would find. They explained that they would probably remove the part of the pancreas where the mole was to test it further and to exclude any possible cancer.

After the 8-hour operation, I woke and found I was cut in an arc shape from left to right across my abdomen and found out that my whole pancreas was removed due to the mole being one of many tumours that had grown all over the pancreas.

From going into hospital, I stayed for a total of 8 weeks. I had an excellent surgeon, whose name was Mr Ashley Dennison, who I cannot thank enough for his help. Mr Dennison is currently a Consultant General Surgeon based at the Leicester General Hospital. He specialises in general and laparoscopic surgery and hepatobiliary and pancreatic surgery.

The pancreas was removed and this is why I am diabetic, as the pancreas produces insulin. If one's pancreas slows down or stops producing insulin, this causes diabetes. I was instantly told I had to inject insulin for the rest of my life and at 20 years old it felt like a big deal and it seemed like the end of the world.

Type 1 diabetics are dependent on insulin because for some reason the pancreas no longer produces it. The pancreas is a gland about 15 cm long that produces insulin. Insulin balances glucose (sugar) levels in the blood. The organs of the body can be seriously damaged by high levels of glucose in the blood. The insulin moves glucose out of the blood and into the cells where it is converted into energy.

The symptoms of diabetes are thirst, tiredness, urinating more frequently and weight loss. The weight loss occurs because the body breaks down fat and muscle to produce energy because there is no glucose in the cells to convert to energy.

Type 1 diabetics have to take insulin all their life combined with regular blood tests and a healthy diet. The fine balance of insulin treatment against diet is learned gradually.

The staff were wonderful and very supportive. I was still very young and found it hard at first to accept this was happening to me. The operation left me with a large scar running from one side of my body to the other. Following the operation the pain was initially intolerable. Again I was so lucky to have the support of great medical staff. The therapists worked with me daily for quite a few months to get me to walk properly again.

It was only 3 years since winning the youth title. I now had a lovely daughter Sophie at home and here I was trying to get to grips with what to me was a debilitating illness.

From this day on in darts, from local leagues to the professional circuit, Jabba became my nickname, because I had to inject myself daily.

I remember whilst in hospital I was preparing to play in the Embassy Gold Cup. Whilst in Occupational Therapy I had made a backboard with a chalk board, a bracket and a dartboard that my dad had brought in for me to practise on. I was practising whilst having a drip in my left arm with a stand!

An interesting fact about the Embassy was that in 1993, the 16th annual running of this event was the last time it was staged as a unified tournament. John Lowe beat Alan Warriner in the final. At that time there was still on offer a £51,000 bonus for a nine-dart finish. It was, incidentally, not claimed. Gosh I wish I had been there!

I recall the hype that was created around the Embassy of 1993 as plans were in place for the PDC (then known as the World Darts Council WDC), to have patches on the players' shirts. The BDO told them to remove the patches, which almost caused players to boycott the event as their futures could now be in doubt.

It must have been quite a sight and it is something that got me by in hospital, being able to go down to Occupational Therapy to practise for an hour twice a day.

I think when the Gold Cup finals where played at Trentham Gardens, Stoke-on-Trent, I was beaten in the early rounds. I was very low in energy and very tired as it was only a couple of weeks after I had come out of hospital.

Stoke seems to have an ability to produce great darts players like Phil Taylor, Adrian Lewis, Ted Hankey, Chris Mason (who lived for a couple of years in Stoke), Andy Hamilton and Ian White to name but a few.

The effects of the operation do not affect me now except that I have to take medication for my diabetes, although for the initial period after coming out of hospital following major abdominal surgery I was unable to walk unaided for around 6 months.

My parents were with me when I went down for the surgery and I knew they were worried for me. Although I was not a child and I had moved out of the family home, it was almost as though they still thought I was a baby. I guess they were just being parents.

I take two types of insulin: one type is three injections during the day, and the other one for the night time. I used to take Humulin Soluble during the day, which is a quick-acting one, and Humulin Isophane, which is a cloudy substance that is slow-releasing insulin to regulate blood sugar levels slowly while you sleep.

My medication changed as recently as 12 months ago. I now take Nova Rapid, which is more common, quick-releasing insulin for during the day and Glargine for night time. These are two more advanced brands of insulin than either of the Humulin variety.

I also use a blood test monitor, which helps me keep check of my blood sugars. At present they average around 8.0 mmols, which is not too bad. Anywhere between 5 and 9 is where I like to keep it. If it is too low, I need sugary foods and drinks to bring it back. If it is too high, a couple of units of insulin help me to bring it down.

Since the operation in 1996 I have been a type 1 diabetic as I have no way of producing insulin. I currently have to inject myself on a regular basis. I think most diabetics have to inject themselves a couple of times a day. As I do not produce any insulin whatsoever, then for me it is four times a day.

I have to be honest, and certainly in the early days it has made a significant change to my lifestyle. I have always enjoyed a beer and a fair proportion of junk food. I have to moderate this now and control my blood sugar levels by the measured application of the insulin injections.

I had to return to the Leicester General Hospital annually for a decade for check-ups to see that there was no return of the tumours anywhere else. I have now been discharged as there have been no further growths discovered.

Living with diabetes

Obviously living with diabetes is a demand that needs total attention. If it is not well controlled everything goes out of synchronisation, including focus and concentration; two attributes that are essential in darts. I cope with it by being a good boy, so to speak. Not to drink too much or eat the wrong food and getting appropriate exercise etc.

I have been in touch with Diabetes UK, as they are going to be a charity I will be working with during 2013, along with LOROS. LOROS actually stands for Leicestershire and Rutland Organisation for the Relief of Suffering. It is a local charity here in Leicester providing care and support for the county. The charity does not charge and therefore relies on fundraising to finance its wide range of care and facilities.

I deal with my medical condition on a day-to-day basis. To be honest in the world of professional darts it does not make a difference. I have an injection in the morning before breakfast, one at lunchtime and one before my evening meal, then one before bed. The only thing that may differ slightly is the time of the evening meal. If it is a long day competing, then my evening meal may be slightly later than normal.

Clearly there are other areas I have to watch and I have a view on, for example my opinion on drugs; I can honestly say I have never used drugs. I have seen what they do to people and constantly hear the way they destroy people's lives. Is it really worth it? I do not think so and I will do what I can to persuade youngsters to steer clear of them.

Personally, I think alcohol is okay in moderation. I have a bit myself when competing. I do not think alcohol cures nerves or the like, but what I find it does is it keeps the focus. My focus is easily hindered so I find a couple of beers keeps my concentration up.

I have never been a smoker. I do not have any negativity towards smokers because it is their own decision to smoke or not. I actually think the national smoking ban has been the main reason the pub trade has been hit so hard.

Not related to the diabetes, I started to suffer in 1997 from too much calcium and anaemia. I was back in hospital again and diagnosed with parathyroid disease. This is over-activity of one of the parathyroid lobes, which can cause an imbalance in calcium. The possible effects are osteoporosis and kidney stones. Like many, the only real treatment for me was the removal of the offending glands.

For me this was a 2-day visit to the Leicester Royal Infirmary where I had my parathyroids, which sit on the corners of thyroid gland, removed. It was quite a simple procedure. This has left me with a second large scar across my throat and neck. Fortunately no more medication this time.

I am not sure what the implications would have been if I had not had this operation.

Jamie and Bradley

In my early twenties I'd had two young daughters, Sophie and Molly, though their mother and I separated after 4 years and I moved back in with my parents who said that they saw it coming and were alright with me moving back.

In 1999 I met Sonia Norman. She worked behind the bar at the Nautical William where I played darts. We have two wonderful sons Jamie who was born in 2002 and Bradley, late in 2003.

All four of my children – Christmas 2012

I really do not know why but after about 4 years together Sonia and I separated and I lived on my own for a while. Both boys are so supportive of me and I try to see them on a weekly basis.

During this time I lived on the Saffron Lane estate with my parents before and after my first partner, then Wigston Harcourt with the boys' mum. Then I had my own flat in Aylestone. All of these are in Leicester.

When I was 20 I had my pancreas removed which resulted in diabetes and I was on disability benefit for a couple of years. After I recovered from my abdominal surgery, I worked with my daughters' grandfather who ran Kibworth and Loughborough recycling sites.

In my late 20s, I took a computer course as this seemed to be the way the future would pan out. With my pass I went for an interview at the Inland Revenue (now HMRC) and after a shortlist test I received a phone call to say I could have the job, which began in October 2002. I worked on the New Tax Credits team.

I played for the school football team, but only during my early years at junior level. I played pool at the local youth club in my very early teens. Although now I purely concentrate on playing darts.

I did nevertheless support Liverpool FC. I still do to this day. My granddad was from there and from the age of 8 onwards I went to Anfield quite a few times. I remember going to Leicester City FC's old stadium at Filbert Street and Notts County's Meadow Lane as well to watch the Reds many years ago.

The death of my mother

In August 1999 my mother Carole was diagnosed with cancer of the oesophagus. My mum was the only one in my family who smoked and I do not suppose that helped. I am not sure she fully stopped but she did try. It was always in the kitchen. The oesophagus is the medical name for the gullet; the tube carrying food from the throat to the stomach. Symptoms include difficulty in swallowing, weight loss, throat pain and coughing. It is more common in men. Smoking and drinking are risk factors.

It is difficult to cure as there are no symptoms in the early stages and by the time they occur the cancer may have already spread to nearby tissue.

I think dad smoked in his early twenties but suffered from myeloma leukaemia and stopped straight away and never touched another cigarette.

I am not sure if she knew before this and was just keeping it from the family. I well remember the day when she told us. The three of us children were back in the house with dad when mum spoke with us. Mum said she had to go into hospital for chemo. Mum said she was going to fight it for the family and she was going to be okay and not to worry.

Mum was still working in the local supermarket, but on reduced hours. Dad immediately quit his job to look after her. He was a builder at that time.

She seemed to get ill quickly after that. Her hair fell out and she lost loads of weight. Mum said though when she went to the hospital to have the chemotherapy sessions she could actually feel it working on the cancer. This seemed reassuring. Mum was a bit poorly after the sessions at the hospital.

A few months later it was Christmas and just after that mum informed us that the cancer had spread. This seemed so quick as she had only told us about it in the August just gone.

The eve of the new millennium was a strange time for me. Many people were making plans for what they wanted to achieve and personally I still had the dream of becoming a pro darts player. But personally, my life was not great. I was in between jobs working for different recruitment agencies, I was a single father in my early twenties with two daughters and my own mum's days were running out as she was losing her battle with cancer. I did not really feel like it was an exciting part of my life and suggested I see it out at home with my mum and dad.

My mum, being the woman she was, told me to go and party so I did go out although it was not for much after midnight.

When my mum passed away on the 22nd February 2000, it was a very sad time, but I was relieved that she could rest and now be pain free. One of our last conversations was about me fulfilling my potential to earn a living on the dartboard. I know she would be very proud of me.

In January 2000 mum started going to LOROS for respite. It was only for a few days at a time but it seemed good for her and it gave dad a rest. Our friends were great and there was never a problem getting a lift when we needed it.

Mum was very protective, especially of her children and she did not want us to come with her on the visits to LOROS. With her hair falling out mum got a wig. My cousin Susan bought the wig.

I remember a Wednesday morning in February when she said she did not feel right, but not really feeling poorly. She had been on the phone to LOROS and they asked mum to come in. Dad went with her but mum told us to go to work and she would see us later. They sent an ambulance, as she was at the time very weak.

I received a call at lunchtime from my brother who wanted me to go home because mum was not well.

When I got back my brother was at home and my sister was at LOROS with my dad.

I had arranged to get a lift from one of the ladies at the shop where my mum worked at three that afternoon to go and see her. I was in their bedroom getting some clothes when the phone rang. My brother took the call and then said to me that she had gone. I am not sure who the call was from. I thought he meant my lift and I said that was okay and I would get the bus instead. I do not know why I thought that. "No it's mum," he said, "she's gone." I think I was expecting it, but mum was only 48! It was still a massive shock.

Dad and my sister stayed with her for some time that day; I did not go to the hospital chapel to see mum. I wanted to remember her as she was. Since seeing my dad in the hospital chapel, I now wish I had gone to see mum.

That first evening after she passed away the house was full of friends and relatives; mum was a very popular lady. I remember my auntie Jean came around and my nanna and people were coming all evening expressing their condolences and their disbelief that Carole had gone.

We had planned already to have a fundraiser in April with Eric Bristow and this still went ahead and the money raised was donated to the baby care unit at the Leicester Royal Infirmary.

The funeral was soon after and mum was laid to rest in a family plot at Saffron Hill Cemetery. This was alongside my mum's dad, my granddad. I still visit the grave on a regular basis as I miss my mum very much.

Debbie

By 2002 I was working for the Inland Revenue in Leicester. Darts was going well and even though I was back on my own there was a balance and drive to my life.

In the early part 2003 I went through to the Inland Revenue darts regional play-offs. Here I bumped into Debbie who, like me, made it through to the finals on that day.

I won the men's and Debbie won the ladies. We first spoke at the presentation. It was not until the National Finals in Nottingham later that year that I saw her again. We became good friends.

We often saw each other at dart events and works nights out. Over time Debbie's marriage came to an end and my relationship with Sonia ended. Our friends often teased us about getting together, but we just laughed it off.

I asked Debbie out for a drink away from friends and she accepted, even saying she was 10 years older than me, as if this mattered. We continued meeting once or twice a month and this seemed to work quite well. It was quite difficult even though we worked for the same employer, as we lived in different cities and I was playing darts.

In 2008 after my World Championships debut we moved in together, but not until I had met her children and was given the seal of approval. I then had to pass the possible future mother-in-law test. Debbie chose her mum's 60th birthday to introduce us. Christina Varney welcomed me into the family with "If you hurt our Deborah I'll thump you". I had been accepted into the Varney family.

We had built a solid relationship and now I was a bit older I was able to take things slower and choose the right path.

Debbie and me

We had talked about marriage a few times and that was as far as it went. Debbie was due to be bridesmaid for her friends Joanne and Steve. The more they discussed their wedding, the more we talked about us possibly marrying. It was on a visit to Joanne and Steve's reception venue that we both said how nice it would be for us to get married there.

A few days later while Debbie was in the bath, I took the plunge and rang Debbie's dad George and asked if he had any objection to us getting married. He said he was more than happy. So I went into the bathroom and proposed whilst Debbie was in the bath. She said yes and we both burst into fits of laughter due to the circumstances in which I had asked her.

The following month we were in Leicester and had just walked by Goldsmiths Jewellers. There was this one ring that just stood out and we both liked it. I said if it fitted I would buy it for her. It fitted and just in time, as they were about to close the shutters.

We planned the wedding for the following year and the actual date being 15th August 2009. We chose that weekend as the PDC tour was in Canada and I had no intention of travelling to that event.

We were married in St Werburgh's Church in Spondon, near Derby. Our guests included players and family from the darts world; Colin and Sarah Osborne, Chris and

Lorna Mason, Kirk Shepherd and Emma Harris, Chris and Winnie Sargent amongst them. Chris was our photographer for the wedding. We were married by Vicar Eleanor Berry.

St Werburgh's Church in Spondon

The Vicar of Saint Werburgh's Spondon, Fr. Julian Hollywell SCP, kindly allowed us to use the following words from his website, which describe the history.

"The present church dates back to around 1390, when it was completed to replace an earlier church destroyed by fire, along with almost the entire village in 1340. It is a very large church compared with the size of the village as it was in the fourteenth century.

"The earlier church must have been equally large because the present church stands on its foundations. Spondon is an outer suburb of the city of Derby and the church should not be confused with the city centre church of St. Werburgh, which at present is semi-redundant. St. Werburgh's in Spondon stands at the top of a hill on the north side of the river Derwent and in the centre of the original village."

A great church and we thank the Reverend Julian Hollywell for the history of this beautiful venue for our special event.

Our honeymoon was again aligned to a gap in the PDC calendar with a week in Tenerife later in the year. Debbie's parents were very happy, especially her dad George (Varney), who used to play regularly alongside darting legend John Lowe. George is very well respected and currently still plays for the George and Dragon in the Belper Darts League.

Debbie is a great help to me as a professional player. She is able to help me organise my diary and ensure I am aware of what is coming up. I think now at exhibitions Debbie really comes in to her own.

When we get to a venue Debbie will start the organising. Firstly making sure the room is set up properly. I like to make sure the sponsors' tables are in place, Debbie will ensure that all the literature and goodies are distributed. Gaz also has started to learn the ropes, which enables us to provide a professionally run evening.

Quite often I am trying to blend talking to the early punters and the players that will be helping with the exhibition. Most of the time I can remember the names of the guests, especially those I have played with over the years. Debbie helps the times I forget. Also it is important commercially to make sure all the merchandise is on display and someone is manning the desk and that is often Debbie. A very good partnership I think.

Sometimes at exhibitions I get carried away with chat. Debbie quickly reminds me of why I am there and points me towards the dartboard. She regularly does this at home too, as I can sometimes be lazy when practice is concerned.

We have done some nights at Eyres Monsell over the last few years as a way of thanking them for helping me start out in 1989. Besides me, players have included: Adrian Lewis, Kevin Painter, Paul Nicholson, Andy Hamilton, Colin Osborne, Eric Bristow, John Lowe, Peter Manley and Bob Anderson.

Sponsors have included: Mr Tax Limited, Wigston Blinds and the breweries of the clubs.

Local darts

Success in local darts has been in excess of 320 trophies obtained over 15 years played locally. Around 40 league singles, 30 league pairs, 50 league winners and 30 league cups.

This picture was taken as I started to play again after pancreatic surgery. Pictured with the World Youth Championship Trophy.

To date, in open tournaments, I have competed in around 200 finals and 130 singles titles. One world title (youth) 5 professional titles, 3 major television quarter-finals and 8 competitive 9-darters. One on the professional tour against Simon Whitlock – Crawley 2010: 167, 180, 154 (t20, t20, d17).

Mondays – Leicester Inner City Darts League, 1990 to 1992 – played for Eyres Monsell with my dad who won the 180s. We finished runners-up in my first season. Opposition – Scraptoft Valley.

Years 1992 to 1997 – Central Invitation DL. I played for Eyres Monsell early on and then The Nautical William. League and cup wins and singles, pairs and threes wins in what was classed as Leicester's toughest darts league around the early 1990s. Opposition – Beaumont Leys as well as EMWMC, Nautical William depending on who I played for.

This league folded in 1997 and CEDL was formed. I did not play in the first season of CEDL as it was fairly small and nobody knew how it would go, and with the venue being on the other side of town and me working shifts made it virtually impossible for me.

I did not join until the following 1998/99 season where I finished 6th, losing 19 of my 66 games. In the first season only 15 players entered. Each player played each other three times, with knockout singles and pairs competitions during the season. Prize money was worked out for all 15 players to receive something back, plus cash for monthly award winners, highest finishes and most 180s. The majority of these were accompanied by annual trophies.

It was a success, with other players turning up each week just to see how it was it all working out, and enjoying it that much they were signing up for the second year.

Presentation night was packed with Roland Scholten being invited to do an exhibition with the players from the league, as well as presenting the awards for the first season, including the winner's trophy and a cheque for £500 to Ricky Sudale.

Ricky works for DHL and is still active in Leicestershire darts. Roland used to live and run the Danish Invader pub in Stamford Lincolnshire. Roland used to play local Superleague darts for Ketton and is still ranked in the PDC top 50.

As the league was in the upstairs function room of the club and with only four free-standing boards used in the first year, they knew they had to move to the concert room and purchase four more free-standing boards. They did, and with good publicity circulating around the

County the second season of the Belgrave Liberal singles Darts League had now grown to 32 members.

Two more committee members were recruited as the amount of work involved became too much for Ian and Lee. They were Karen Roberts and the well-respected Leicestershire County Secretary, Diane Clarke.

Ladies also wanted to join, and instead of having a separate league, there was no objection to ladies and men playing against each other as equals. They knew they were improving all the time and by asking the players for their comments and ideas on how they saw the league progressing. They knew that whatever changes were made, they had the approval and backing of the league's members.

I came second in 1999/2000 losing out to Ricky Sudale on leg difference as we both finished with the same number of points. This was the year that Sean Reed from Australia also played in the CEDL before returning to Japan/Australia. Sean also competed in the 2012 ladbrokes.com World Championship losing to Justin Pipe in round one.

In 2000/2001 I also came second this time to Jez Porter by two points. In 2001/2002 I won my first 78 games (a feat which will never be beaten).

Lee Saville and Alan White were the only players that season (98 games) to beat me as I won my first CEDL title in great style.

In 2002/2003, I retained my title losing only eight matches. I then took a 3-year break as my boys were only babies and I had to think of them first.

In 2006/2007 I came third. In my final year 2007/2008 I won for the third time losing only five games.

It was coming towards the end of the 2007/08 CEDL season and with only one point needed to secure the title I came up against a relative newbie in the Leicester darting scene, Tim Kirby. Feeling relaxed as ever during warm-up I joked with Tim that if he should just let me have the one leg I needed to win the league that would be great but then he could have the win. Fully expecting a win it was a shock when Tim went off like a train and took the first leg. At this point I turned to Tim and said "I was only joking about you having the win but I do want the one leg".

After a little laugh between us I proceeded to get back in gear and ran out the winner 3-1. During that season another local league player Leigh Peet actually did the double over me and this just goes to show the strength and depth of talent there is out there and with dedication how far some players could go.

In total I played for seven seasons, with 590 total matches played, 528 games won and losing only 62, a win rate of almost 90 per cent. I also scored a total of 164 maximum 180s, and recorded two 170 finishes.

I continue to sponsor the CEDL, and very often pop in to see old friends. I am also a supporter of the CEDL chosen charity "wishes4kids".

The league has gone from strength to strength. It is now housed at the Enderby Social Club and the Spot On in Loughborough. There are over 100 players and top prizes of around £1000 for the league winners. If I had time I would not mind playing in the league again as it has such a high calibre of players on their books.

Tuesdays is the Everards Darts League. This league had a good team format of 4 pairs, 2 fours and an 8-a-side. It was one of Leicester's most popular leagues in the 1990s and the noughties. Scott Hopewell and I won the pairs in 1990 when we were both aged 14!

I won the league with Eyres Monsell quite a few times as well as winning the cups, singles, pairs threes and fours, along with the highest finish and the most 180s. There were lots of memorable nights. Opposition was The Glen, Notts Oddfellows, Newfoundpool and the West End. I think I won the most 180s in 1993 at the age of 17.

Fridays I played for EMWMC in the Leicester Trades League. Just one leg of pairs straight start and an 8-a-side leg in the early days of a very quick league. Opposition was the Post Office and the Coach and Horses.

In 2001 playing for the Eyres Monsell Club I was partnered with Sonia and we beat John Gibson and Lee Gibson in the final of the Pollard Bowl. In 2003 I was partnered this time with Dave Parkinson and again in the same competition we beat, in the final, Alan Hogg and Steve Trigg.

In 2003, still in the old Trades League we won the Colin Merrall Triples. My teammates that night were Lee Peet and Bob Watt. We managed to overcome a good team of John Gibson, Steve Trigg and Ramish Patel.

In the same year I was also part of the winning team in the Walkers Crisps Fours. We had a strong team of Dave Parkinson, Dave Hayes, John Bownes and me. The opposition that night were Dave Randall, Bob Watt, Lee Peet and Mick O'Hara.

Open singles at The Ship Inn were played on a Friday night; usually lots of good Superleague and County players would attend as ideal practice for Superleague the next day.

Superleague on Saturday afternoons: Eyres Monsell, Cosby, Leicester North. I played from the age of 15, and after four matches I was selected for the County as a reserve. I hold one of the highest Superleague averages in Leicestershire Superleague history. Against Earl Shilton (17, 12, 12) 36.66 average (109.98).

Highest average for Leicestershire County 37.58 (14, 14, 12) (112.74) (100, 140, 140, 113, 8 in 2) (99, 140, 140, 90, 32 in 2) (140, 180, 170, 11 in 3).

I played around 80 times for Leicestershire and eight times for Cambridgeshire. In 2001 I registered for Cambridgeshire Superleague and played for the Nags Head at Peterborough; within a few weeks I was selected for the County and got Man of the match, away against Hampshire in my debut in the BICC Premier Division.

I was then in the 'A' team for the remainder of the season, but the following year I returned to Leicestershire. I only had one season for Cambridgeshire in the premier league; I gave it a season to see if I was good enough.

The thing with me is I like to push myself, to see if I can make the grade; if not try and try until you get there.

My debut was against Newmarket who were the team to beat. I was last on against Shaun Greatbatch son of Sandra. Shaun was current Gold Cup pairs champion with Mervyn King. I beat Shaun 3-0 with a 32.67 average. Other Newmarket players were Mervyn King and Ian Brand. Cambridgeshire Superleague men's was then the best of seven matches.

The senior game

I am fortunate to have some great sponsors: Unicorn, the biggest name in Darts. I joined Unicorn in June 2009 as I was previously with Red Dragon and my contract had expired in the April. Debbie and I had arrived home from Bolton after I had reached the quarter-finals of the UK Open losing to practice partner Colin Osborne and we were going through emails and Facebook messages when a certain Mr Edward Lowy (Unicorn Managing Director) popped up on Facebook chat.

After a 15-minute chat I was being sent a contract with the best darts company in the world and life as a darts professional does not get any better than that.

Matt Rankin is player liaison officer and he makes sure I have what I need, when I need it. He is worth his weight in gold and I find myself very fortunate to be part of such an elite team.

I currently use 23 gram Unicorn Jamie Caven Scalloped Contender darts, which I have been very fortunate to have designed myself, with the expert help of Alex Ross. My current walk on song is 'Tom Hark' by the Piranhas.

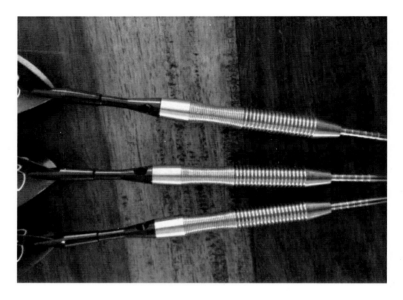

My latest darts from Unicorn

The scallop is where my forefinger and thumb sit so I know I hold the darts correctly each time.

This has all been possible due to my decision to enter the professional game in 2007. This is never an easy choice and there are probably many of you reading this wishing you had given it a go.

I am not saying it is easier to get on the circuit today, but just different. The PDC has a very structured tour approach that allows you to conduct your business in an extremely professional and planned manner.

Action shot 2012

I would imagine if I had been born a few generations ago, it would have been so different. Players who choose to make their living from playing darts would have had lots of avenues to pull the money in.

Sponsorship would have been a key factor or mates and family who were prepared to help. As well as entering money tournaments, there would be exhibitions and probably the after game matches for wagers.

I am not sure how Debbie would feel if I came home and said I had lost my tournament winnings in a winner-takes-all cash game at the end of the night. They were brave players I think in those days.

Today I am able to plan my schedule and build in exhibition and charity nights around the professional tour.

For me this all started in November 2006 when I had just played Phil Taylor at a local tournament staged at the Notts Oddfellows Club.

Peter Clare, from Mr Tax Ltd, offered me some sponsorship and Phil Taylor suggested that I should join the PDC circuit as this was the right time. At this time I was practising about 2 or 3 hours a day at the Eyres Monsell WMC. I was hoping to make an early impression once I hit the professional game.

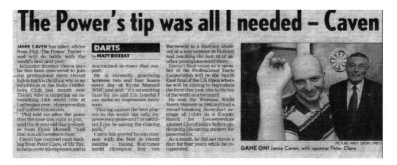

The start of my professional career and thanks to the Leicester Mercury

With about 15 professional events played in the 2007 PDC circuit I entered the World Championship PDPA qualifiers. I won through to be one of the eight qualifiers on the night. My television debut at the Alexandra

Palace saw me beat Wes Newton in straight sets and although I lost to Wayne Mardle in the second round, I believe I had made an impression.

After the first round win against Wes, myself and Debbie returned to Derby to make plans to return to London but needed a change of clothes and some more medication etc.

We bought every national newspaper on that morning hoping to see the result of my win printed in them. In the *Daily Mirror* was a two-page spread about this phenomenon with one eye that had won on the world stage.

It was a very strange feeling. On the tube sat across from us was a lady flicking through the *Daily Mirror* and we guessed she was on that very page as we received a double take as she kept peering over the top of the page.

We returned to London the next day with Debbie's son for my game against Wayne. Although gutted about my loss I was still upbeat on the train journey home. Opposite were a couple who kept staring. I smiled and thought they recognised me. I liked this new-found fame.

As we pulled into one of the stations the lady looked over and said "I know you don't I?" I said "Yes you probably do", to which the reply was, "No not you" and pointed to Gaz. "Are you the drummer at Pride Park?"

(Derby County football club). To which Debbie and Gaz burst into fits of laughter. She was right about Gaz and I came down to earth with a bump.

John Gwynne, who commentated on my TV debut win over Wes Newton along with Dave Lanning, reminded me shortly after the victory of the time in Bristol in 2004 when I won the civil service national singles championship, as he compared the final. He had asked me at the time about my ambition. I told him simply, I want to be a top professional in the PDC within the next few years. It is funny how things sometimes turn out and we occasionally reminisce about this conversation.

Alexandra Palace is situated in North London and has been a major venue for all sorts of activities for over 130 years.

I then had three runs in the professional tour taking me to the last 16. Then I qualified for the UK Open in Bolton. I made it to the second round where I lost to Steve Smith.

I then reached my first final at the Welsh UK Open Regional Final in September, losing to the 'Rocket' Ronnie Baxter. I also made a semi-final of a Player Championship in Dublin before being beaten by Raymond van Barneveld and a quarter-final in Killarney.

For the Dublin game we arrived a day early at 'The City West' which was our first time at this impressive venue.

It was and still is the home of the World Grand Prix and although I have competed in that event three times, I was only there for the Player Championships on this occasion. After an early flight, we arrived and checked into the hotel quite early in the day, and as we found an old sock in the room, myself and Debbie were upgraded with posh smellies, a fruit basket, a bathrobe each and some slippers!

After some lunch we had a nap in the afternoon as we were up early for the 6am flight and Debbie woke to find me having some sort of seizure. She then ran to reception to get an ambulance which took us to Tallaght hospital. My bloods levels were checked and after some glucose I soon came round. After a review I soon learned my diabetes medication needed updating, and after several hours we returned to the hotel.

After a check-up at the hospital due to her limping, it was evident that Debbie had torn her Achilles tendon from running to the reception to get help; so it was an eventful day. Needless to say I needed to prepare for the weekend's events, and the hospital visit did not seem to be too much hindrance as on the Sunday I reached the semi-finals losing out 3-1 in sets to Raymond Van Barneveld.

These results ensured I got a World Championship return through the player championship order of merit. My attempt though to win a Grand Slam of Darts was halted when I lost at the semi-final stage of the ITV wild card qualifier.

In 2009 at the Alexandra Palace I again played well but lost narrowly to Mark Walsh in round one. I then achieved a semi-final run in the UK Open North-East Regional Final before suffering a first round exit to Colin Lloyd in the Player Championship Finals.

Two PDC Professional Tour quarter-finals followed in April before I claimed my first professional win. I defeated Alan Tabern 6-5 in the UK Welsh Regional Final in Newport. I do like Wales.

In the UK Open that followed I also had a successful run. I first beat Steve Dolan, then Jelle Klaasen and Alex Roy. I was now in my first televised quarter-final.

My great training partner and friend Colin Osborne was the opponent. On this occasion Colin was too strong for me. I did though reach another player championship final in Barnsley and lost out to Mark Walsh.

I was able to qualify for the Las Vegas Desert Classic where I came up against Phil Taylor in the first round and although I went down 3-6, I was happy with my first

TV ton-plus average. Well anyway it was a lovely part of the world.

In the following World Matchplay at the Winter Gardens I lost in the opening encounter to World number two James Wade.

As autumn approached in September 2009 I won my second Players Championship victory. I was triumphant over Steve Beaton and picked up £6000 prize money for the second time that year. I was also able then to qualify for the World Grand Prix. This is a double start competition but I was edged out by Wes Newton in the early stages although it cemented my top 32 World ranking.

Action shot 2012

My progression continued with qualification for the European Championships. I took out Terry Jenkins in the first round and then lost to Jelle Klaasen in round two. This meant automatic qualification into the World Championships for the third successive year.

Gary Anderson, however, ended my hopes in this competition with a three two loss. I felt nonetheless I was maintaining my consistency as I headed towards the end of 2010, as I reached one more final, four semi-finals and three quarter-finals in the build-up to the UK Open in Bolton.

Obviously consistency counts but it was not enough to beat Andy Smith who took me out in the last 32. This was followed by a second appearance at Blackpool where Ronnie Baxter was able to peg me ten legs to seven to see my exit from the competition.

The European Championships that followed allowed me to pick up some ground. I obtained wins over Gary Anderson and Barrie Bates to reach the last eight but finally went out to Terry Jenkins.

Sometimes you just know when your game is good and I took this form with me to Canada. I was able to pick up my third professional win in the London Ontario Players Championship.

The following day I also reached the final but Colin Lloyd prevented it from being a perfect pair.

In September 2010, I hit my first tour 9-darter. Against Simon Whitlock in the semi-finals in Crawley. At 0-1 down I started the second leg with 167. This was followed with a 180 and finished with 154 (t20, t20, d17). Quite an unorthodox way of a perfect leg, but nevertheless it had won me my first silver 9-dart pin at the PDC Awards Dinner, which followed the World Championship final.

My fourth championship came in October that year in Dublin over Ronnie Baxter with a 6-5 win. After winning the Pro Tour event in Dublin 2010, I met Ash Spires. Ash is a member of the Stockport College Darts Academy, and some of the young lads were in Dublin with Paul Mack who helps to run the group. Ash told me he had been diagnosed as diabetic, and was struggling with dealing with it at the time.

After winning I gave him some words of encouragement and we exchanged mobile numbers and email addresses so we could stay in touch. I then saw him in Derby in February 2011 just after I had beaten Adrian Lewis in the final of the Players Championship. I think Ash should attend every event! This is one of the reasons why I decided to write this book, knowing that I can make a difference and inspire others to achieve.

At Alexandra Palace of the same year in the December, was my fourth consecutive World Championship and South African, Devon Peterson was in my way. I won three sets to one with a 161 finish.

This was my first win under a new manager. I was now teamed up with Jess Harding, a former British heavyweight boxer. Once again Colin Osborne prevented me from going further.

By January 2011 I had reached the World's top twenty and started with a 6-1 win over Barrie Bates in the Player Championship Finals before going out to Andy Smith.

My fifth professional win came in February 2011, played in my new home town of Derby with a win over the then World Champion Adrian Lewis. I reached the quarter-final the following day.

During 2011 my form stayed about even with highlights being a quarter-final at the UK Open qualifier in February. I picked up £5k at the World Match Play in July reaching the last 32. Although I was whitewashed by James Wade 10-0, I was at a low point in my career as a bad performance on such a stage is embarrassing since there is nowhere to hide.

The morning after, Debbie had arranged a bit of a meet and greet with a few supporters at a local café. This is the last thing I wanted to do but it proved so very rewarding.

This is where I met Mark Cooper and his family. Mark is one of the nicest people you could ever wish to meet. He has more of my merchandise than I do myself. I also met Wayne North for the first time. Wayne has his own page on Facebook, which is growing very well and is called 'Wayne's World of Darts'. The following month I reached the semi-final of the PDPA Players Championship in Canada.

Me and Mark Cooper

October saw another £4k from the World Grand Prix. The significance of the money is twofold. Firstly it calculates your rankings over a rolling 2-year period. Secondly, and more importantly it pays for your mortgage.

Again in October I got through to the semi-final in Spain playing in the PDPA Players Championships. It included a revenge on James Wade for the whitewash in Blackpool, this time with me winning 6-0.

The start of January 2012 was quite lucrative with a last 64 place in the PDC World Championships. During this year to date I have been achieving a good share of quarter and semi-final places. I need though to continue to convert some of these into final wins to secure my continued ranking position and my own financial security.

This follows a tough few months personally, as my father passed away. He was my best friend and biggest supporter. He travelled the country with me in my early days and was at the foot of the stage when I came off from winning the World Youth back in 1993.

I missed the major events of the World Matchplay, the European Championship and the World Grand Prix, which saw me slide down from 19 to 31 in the rankings in double quick time. But this did not matter to me at the time as the man who was always there for me, was there no more.

Debbie did a great job of getting me back on my feet, being the fantastic woman that she has been since the day we met. This came to light as performances picked up again, including an Irish Masters semi-final spot and a semi-final spot in Killarney.

There was also a great run in the internet-streamed Championship League Darts, where Simon Whitlock beat me in the semi-finals of the whole event, a defeat that meant I had missed out on the Grand Slam of Darts at the final hurdle again.

I managed to win the Coventry Open in November with a ton-plus average in the final. I was still on form and felt good.

Action shot 2012

My father's death

Following the death of my mum, about a year later my dad started to take ill. This was in 2001 and I was aged 25.

Sonia and I moved in with dad for a while just to keep an eye on him. After a while things seemed to settle down. Dad had moved in to a bungalow and Sonia and I got back to family life at home.

Me and my dad

Around 2008 dad started to deteriorate again and he was diagnosed with suffering from dementia. We all had noticed how he had become more vacant and unsteady.

Dementia refers to a group of related symptoms (called a syndrome). It is associated with an ongoing decline of short-term memory, thinking, language, judgement and understanding, and the brain's ability to carry out normal tasks.

Over half a million people in England live with dementia and it usually affects people aged 65 or over; it is mostly caused by damage to the structure of the brain.

My sister Lisa was a rock during this time and spent a lot of time with dad. Often making him his dinners and looking after the house. It was quite difficult for Lisa at this time. Although dad provided much entertainment on his mobility scooter going full speed over sleeping policemen and when he reversed out of Lisa's gate into a neighbour's car. He would state that he did not crash into it, he just manoeuvred into it.

Even though dad was diagnosed with dementia, we as a family were not really sure of the full extent of his illness. There were days when he seemed in great spirit and others where his illness made us sad and worried.

In May 2012 dad moved out of his bungalow and went into a care home. At least now he had full-time attention.

July 2012 I was playing at Crawley in the PDPA Players Championships. The home contacted the family to say that dad had fallen asleep during breakfast and they could not revive him and so called an ambulance.

They said to my sister not to rush but meet them at the Leicester Royal Infirmary. They sounded very calm on the phone. When Lisa got there they informed her that they could not revive dad and he died en route to the hospital. They said he had a heart attack; he was on a machine trying to keep him breathing.

They decided not to tell me whilst I travelled home from Crawley but Debbie called and said she would meet me at the services on the motorway as dad was not well. This was strange as when dad had been ill previously, Debbie had not told me until I had got home. So I instantly knew something was not right.

I was with Colin and we were stuck in traffic. Debbie called again and I could tell she was upset and she was really quiet. I asked if we had lost him and her silence confirmed it. Debbie let Melanie and Sonia know and asked them to tell my children. By the time I got to Leicester I was unable to see my dad at that time due to hospital procedures.

I went straight to see my boys and spoke to my girls later that night. The following day I went to see my dad in the hospital chapel. He looked so young and at peace, his face was pain free.

The cause of death was heart failure, dementia and multiple endocrine neoplasia type 1.

With multiple endocrine neoplasia type 1 tumours in the pancreas, pituitary gland and parathyroid gland are most likely.

Up to then there had been no history of heart problems. Dad was 64 years old when he died and he joined my mum in the family plot at the Saffron Hill Cemetery.

The last I thing I was interested in now was darts. Both my parents had gone and I was unsure of my current direction. I was due to play in Dusseldorf the following week in a cut-off for the World Match Play. This was not going to happen now.

Later that week Debbie broached the subject and we talked it through. She reminded me of the promise I had made to my dad. No matter what, I would continue to play. It still did not feel right but I went and played Brian Woods and lost in the first round 6-5. He was not aware, I think, nor would he have known as I flew back home. If my dad had had a say he would have told me to have done it.

I was short by a few hundred pounds in qualifying for the World Matchplay. This was a potential loss of earnings of around £5k. The next few months were just about me going through the motions as I came to terms with the death of my dad. For one of the few times in my life I thought about why I was playing this game.

I do not know how long I will grieve or if I will ever not expect my dad to walk back through the door. I still have to feed and clothe my family and darts is my job, so I see 2013 as a relaunch of my career.

Today

Life on the pro tour is really tough. The last couple of seasons have seen the inclusion of the youth tour, which has enabled us to have a few weekends off, but in recent years we had 40 plus weekends of the year away!

Action shot 2012

Some months would only allow us to have six or seven nights at home! This means a lot of travelling, which can be really boring, involving spending hours in airports and hotel rooms. The majority of pros play in all events so we are like a very big family, seeing each other at each event.

Then there are exhibitions and practice – darts really is more than a full-time job. Even if we are fortunate to have a lot more time at home, the majority of it is taken up with practice. A lot of the players still play some league darts, whether it is local leagues or Superleague. However, I choose not to even though I probably will do so at some point as it makes for good practice.

The pro tour consists of eight UK Open qualifiers – they count to the UK Open Finals, which are held at Bolton Wanderers' Reebok Stadium, usually the first weekend in June. The top 96 prize money earners go through to the finals, and join amateur qualifiers from Riley's darts zones all over the UK.

In recent years, the event sponsor, Speedy Hire, have had play-offs for their customers to enable them to qualify for the TV event too.

The players ranked 65 to 96, plus ties, and the Riley's and Speedy Hire qualifiers enter the draw at the first round stage, and of course any prelims that may be needed. Players ranked 33–64 join the 32 first-round winners to make 64 in the second round with the 32 winners joining the players ranked 1–32 for the third round.

All rounds are drawn so effectively players ranked 1 and 2 could play each other in the third round. This tournament is nicknamed the FA Cup of darts.

Before 2012 the UK Open qualifiers were only used for the UK Open Finals, but now the qualifiers are included into the pro tour order of merit, which counts towards the other major events: The World Matchplay, World Grand Prix, European Championship, Players Championship Finals and of course The World Championship.

Action shot 2012

All the Players Championships also count towards the other major events and 2012 saw the beginning of a new European Tour. Qualification for the European events has changed to the top 32 in the rolling annual order of merit, with a qualifying event taking place to find 20 PDPA members.

There are also four national winners from the country where the Euro tour is held, with another eight qualifiers coming from the rest of Europe.

The Pro Tour is obviously a must for every player outside the top 32 in the order of merit, because this is the way into the majors. The top 16 are automatically in everything apart from the UK Open, for which they have to qualify like everybody else.

Personally I find it difficult to play on TV because the heat is so immense at times; it is like walking into a sauna, and that statement is not an over-exaggeration. Sometimes it is not so hot, but when you play near the end of the session and the lights have been cooking the stage for several hours, that is when it seems to be at its hottest.

With the heat brings sweat, which drains my blood sugar levels. I am still in a work-in-progress to try to rectify this situation, but it does affect performance whilst I try to find something with which to combat it. When it is not so hot, it is easier to concentrate and get into a nice routine and frame of mind, but when something interrupts your routine it is hard to focus and concentrate and this makes the sport much harder.

It is the same for everybody I guess as the heat brings some discomfort to everyone. When you see the phenomenal success Phil Taylor has had over the last 20 odd years it makes you appreciate it more.

My best performances in majors have been when I have played early. I have had three major quarter-finals to date, and the results seem to have been when playing in the early part of the schedule.

As I say I am constantly practising late and getting my practice room to a temperature that is uncomfortable to help with the process of getting more accustomed with these situations.

Exhibitions are really a fun part of the job, and are really the bread and butter as it is guaranteed income when a booking is completed. From the few pro exhibitions I attended as an amateur, I saw what the pros would do to 'show off', and even tried some things like throwing on one knee (which is really popular amongst pros) and even then it would sometimes go in.

I try to vary my routines in exhibition but it always depends on the opposition as some people want a proper game. Some just want some fun – and that is when it is a good time to do exhibition shots. My exhibition shots have included throwing for doubles on a chair, covering doubles and hitting them (through beer mats), playing on 25s and bulls, and starting and finishing on the same double.

Taken at the darts4heroes competition at Barratts pub in Northampton. Here I used the scallop darts for the very first time. I beat James Richardson in the final with over a hundred average.

I regularly get enquiries for exhibitions and I offer very competitive rates, so most enquiries turn into bookings.

Another way in which I have been able to help other people was through my good friend Mark Cooper. There was a local young lady, Paige Williams who was losing her fight with cancer and was only a toddler. Mark

Hylton and I gave our time to perform a fundraising exhibition in Rhyl in North Wales close to Paige's residence.

Our efforts that night helped raise enough towards Paige's dream holiday to Disneyland before she was taken to heaven away from her young parents, Mike and Becky. Paige will always have a place in my heart and makes what I do more rewarding.

Paige and her family

Today I wear a shirt designed by Benjamin Scrivens. Benjamin contacted me through Facebook for my opinion on his artwork he had created for school, which was a Union Jack with a silhouette of me blended in. This was for his graphic Design GCSE.

It was a very good project so I sent the design to Roger Goswell (www.dartshirt.co.uk) who creates my specialist shirts and he made two with Benjamin's design on the back. One was sent to Benjamin for his final piece and I kept one and wore it on TV as I promised I would do. I still wear shirts with this design as an appreciation for Benjamin's hard work.

Shirt designed by Benjamin Scrivens

Even if we are fortunate to have a lot more time at home, the majority of it is taken up with practice.

Within my practice routines I try to focus more on finishing, as that is the most important part to the sport. I do finishes from 81 to 100, which is where you finish 81 and go to 82. If in three separate attempts at 82 it is not completed, you revert back to 81. This can be very frustrating, especially if you get to 99 and then miss!

I do the 121-up game which a lot of tour players do to warm up. You have nine darts to finish 121 and then go to 122. If you check out a finish it becomes a blocker. A blocker means you cannot drop back below that number as you have already hit it. The objective is to get to and finish 170 to complete the game.

This is a game I have used regularly when practising with Colin Osborne and Kevin Painter. Colin is an ideal practice partner as we live only about 20 minutes apart. Kevin meets me in Leicester on a Tuesday as this is around halfway for the pair of us.

I usually go to Leicester and have time with my two sons on a Tuesday after school, so normally I would meet up with Kev around elevenish and practise until around 3 o'clock. I must give a big shout to Hughie Asher, Barney Kettle and Colin Snoots, who have the unenviable task of marking during practice sessions.

With both Kev and Colin, a lot of competitive legs are played too, which is good for keeping sharp.

A practice routine for scoring is one that Colin introduced to me. It is where you can only score on the 20s. Any format of twenties is okay, whether it's 60 or a 180 or anything in between. You have to reach 1000 points without any darts drifting out of the 20 segment – and it is not as easy as it sounds; give it a try and see!

Another practice game is switch, which is taken from *The Definitive Darts Coaching Manual* (another great book by David Kirby and one that I endorse). Switch is where you have to hit a ton and then double 16 to complete a switch. Then back to a ton and back to double 16. In the book it gives you the option to make your own switches depending on your standard, but when I do it I improve the difficulty as I go.

So I will do a ton, then double 16, and then maybe 140 and then finish on 56. My highest number of switches without missing is 58, and this game alone has helped me get my game back to the standard I want it to be.

Paul Nicholson is another practice partner of mine, although not as much as Kevin or Colin, but he comes to stay at our house on occasion and when he does, we batter the dartboard.

Management is becoming more and more popular in darts. There are quite a few players who have managers now and on tour you see these guys sat at tables with their 'stable' of players. I have recently had a manager over a 2-year contract, which is generally the standard period of management term in darts.

After the 2 years expired, we decided that we could do this ourselves and a manager was not for me as a lot of enquiries come directly to us for exhibitions and sponsorships. For some reason when you mention a manager to an enquirer, a lot of them did not follow it up; I was never sure why.

I seem to be able to keep potential parties interested by dealing with them myself, or through Debbie, as she, along with Gaz, my stepson play a major role in managing me (this is where Team Jabba emerged), whether it be driving me to an exhibition or meeting with companies who show an interest in sponsoring me.

Team Jabba has since become well known over the social media network. We have a full range of our own merchandise displayed at exhibitions and on my website designed by Krispy Brown – www.jamiecaven.co.uk .

Jamie 'Jabba' Caven

Team Jabba

I think when my playing days are over I would like maybe to be an agent or manager of some sort myself.

Youth darts is just as important as we are now seeing in the PDC, where there is an abundance of very talented youth stars coming through the ranks. When I was a youth it was not as big as it is today. I think the future will be even more competitive than it is now and hats off to the PDC for making this happen.

In my early days playing local leagues obviously I started visiting many pubs and clubs around Leicester, which then expanded to the County when I started playing Superleague in 1991.

County darts came pretty soon after so we were travelling the country for away matches, along with knockout competitions that I could afford to go to, but most of them were just around the Midlands.

In 2007 when I decided to give it a go and do the circuit, we still had lots of UK travelling. But many events in Europe included going to Holland and Germany quite a bit – places such as Nuland and Haarlem held Pro Tours, as well as the German cities of Dusseldorf, Berlin and Stuttgart to name but a few.

Northern Ireland held one and Dublin and Killarney still feature as the most popular on the Emerald Isle. I have also been to Gibraltar several times, Canada twice, Atlanta, Georgia and twice to Las Vegas with PDC events.

Financially in the beginning it was very tough, as I could only manage to do what I could afford, but I was working then as well so practice was very limited.

In 2008 I went full time with £7000 behind me that I won at the World Championship. It was a 6-month trial period and if things did not go to plan and the money dried up I would need to return to work.

With careful planning to cover costs, and constantly picking up prize monies on the pro tour it enabled me to continue. Then qualifying for the big events was where the bigger money comes in.

Then as I started to be more recognised a few sponsors came along so it began to get easier to earn a living.

It is a case of all or nothing really – if you are doing well more sponsors and exhibitions come in, if you are not doing so well and need funds the harder things are to come by.

Recently I have been joined by Lee Kavanagh on some of my exhibitions. Lee is a young magician known as Kavano, and was introduced to me during a darts exhibition in Cumbria during 2012.

Lee did a surreal card trick on me that was unbelievable. I picked a card and then he spread the pack over a pool table. I then had to hit the ball off two cushions and turn the card over closest to the ball, which I did and it turned out to be the card I chose. It was unreal.

I think the said trick can be found on YouTube under the search of Kavano Magician. Lee also has a large following on twitter too – @KavanoMagician. He has since worked at darts shows with other players including Kevin Painter and Adrian Lewis.

Since going professional, it has paid for my wedding to Debbie and we moved into a bigger house in 2010.

Most diabetics will probably say the same: you need to look after yourself as best you can to enable your life to be as easy as possible. If it goes out of control, it means more problems: you feel lethargic, tired, run-down, pins and needles, snappy, loss of focus and concentration – so to answer I guess as long as it is all kept under control, the longer and better both will be.

I get tweets and Facebook messages from time to time saying how I have inspired people. I find it quite humbling. The press bring it up from time to time but I do not make a big deal of it.

I have not owned any vehicles as I do not drive. I do not know if actually the eye thing would prevent me from driving but even as a kid I was never really bothered about cars. Maybe it is an inner thing being wary of the blind eye, but really I do not know.

Today my music is as before I like a variety of stuff. I do not follow any singer or group in particular, although a couple of years ago I went to see The Pussycat Dolls in Nottingham with Rihanna supporting them! It was a really good show. Very nice!

Over the next 10 years, I would like to be in a major final at least. I think a final is a celebration of hard work, rather than an all or nothing. Do not get me wrong I would not be satisfied with just getting to a final but how can you be considered a loser if you are beaten only by the guy who has not lost at all?

If I was not playing darts now, what would I do? I do not really know, maybe I would look at some kind of commentary or managerial role within the sport. I would not turn my back on it completely.

The advice I would give to youth/pub players and those wishing to go professional give it a go! Unless you try you will never know. Nevertheless it does not happen overnight.

I know there are lots of players with potential to do very well if they have the chance. But they have no patience. They want it now and are not prepared to work at it. There are players that have a certain talent that may possibly expand if they have the right attitude.

Me with Adrian Lewis at Crawley 2013

Another new sponsor of mine is Kevin Tucker. I first spoke to Kev through double16.com and soon saw his passion for darts, not just as a fan as he wanted to put exhibitions and shows on around his home town of Hartlepool. He enquired about sponsoring me for the World Championship of 2013 to advertise his events on my shirt as at the time he had a joint venture with a friend of putting these shows together.

At Alexandra Palace I met Kev for the first time along with his wife, Fiona and it has to be said they are a genuinely lovely couple whose passion for darts is huge. Soon after Kev informed me that his solo events venture was about to take off, and after some discussion K Tucker Events Management had agreed to sponsor me for 2013.

I have also had the pleasure of meeting Jimmy Anderson at a black tie dinner darts night in 2011 at the Lancashire Cricket Club. Jimmy is at the heart of the England cricket team and in my opinion the best bowler in the world.

We speak regularly on Twitter and he delighted Natalie at Christmas 2012 when he sent her a signed photograph. He is a keen darts fan too and goes to major events when he can. Mark Selby is another popular sportsperson who loves his darts and like me he is from Leicester and is good friends with Kevin Painter.

After meeting Dave Gorman who presented the European Championships in 2010 played at Dinslaken, Germany, we regularly keep in contact and I noticed he was at the Derby Assembly rooms doing a tour of the UK. I contacted him as he tweeted one time of having a dartboard backstage somewhere.

I got in touch with Unicorn who supplied an on-tour set-up. Debbie and I presented Dave with this and to this day he still takes his Unicorn on tour wherever he goes.

Occasionally when myself and Debbie do our shopping at Asda or Morrisons, we are sometimes stared at. Certainly if I have recently been in the local newspaper. Sometimes I am asked for a photograph or signature, which is fine, but it amazes Debbie how people look in the trolley to see what we purchase! We sometimes play a game to see how many times people will look in as a bit of fun!

Do I have any regrets? Regret is a big word. You cannot alter the past so regret is being hard on yourself. If I have done something that I would like to change, I would just do my utmost to rectify it next time.

Now I am in my 30s I live with my wife Debbie, who is my inspiration. She works hard and gives everything 100 per cent. I have four children (two girls and two boys) from previous relationships, who I adore and see regularly. I do not see my daughters as much as I would like, but they are growing up fast and my eldest will soon be out of her teens so that will change pretty soon I think. I have three of the best step-kids anyone could have: Natalie, Gareth and Alex. They all support me in the way I could only wish for.

… onwards and upwards …

Finally it would not be fitting if I did not say a few more words about Peter Clare. Peter passed away towards the end of 2012. This came as such a shock to me because his drive, passion for his work and life (especially his grandsons) seemed limitless.

He has always been there for me since I turned professional, and the year leading up to turning pro his company Mr Tax Ltd, were my first sponsors and he installed the belief to live the dream, certainly in my first year when it seemed such a long way away.

His favourite phrases included "You only get out what you put in" and "You have to visually see yourself hitting the winning double to be world champion". The latter is something I have not managed to do yet, but is very much work-in-progress.

Peter was a very genuine and generous man. He was very supportive of my career and offered me much guidance – he was much more than my accountant. He will be very sadly missed, and it is much thanks to him that I have achieved so much already.

Thank you to all my family, close friends, colleagues and everybody else who have supported me throughout my career to date.

I really hope you have enjoyed this book and with me look forward to sharing some great times together as we move forward.

Jamie

Senior results

Pro Tour Finals during my career so far:

When	Where	Result	Opponent
Sept 2008	Newport, Wales	L 0-3	Ronnie Baxter
May 2009	Newport, Wales	W 6-5	Alan Tabern
June 2009	Barnsley, England	L 4-6	Mark Walsh
Sep 2009	Salzburg, Austria	W 6-2	Steve Beaton
Mar 2010	Wigan, England	L 0-6	Phil Taylor
Aug 2010	Ontario, Canada	W 6-3	Michael Van Gerwen
Aug 2010	Ontario, Canada	L 1-6	Colin Lloyd
Oct 2010	Dublin, Ireland	W 6-5	Ronnie Baxter
Feb 2011	Derby, England	W 6-2	Adrian Lewis
Mar 2013	Wigan England	L 4-6	Robert Thornton

Major quarters run:

UK Open 2009, Bolton, England:

Round	Result	Opponent
3	9-1	Steve Dolan
4	9-6	Jelle Klaasen
5	9-3	Alex Roy
Qtr	3-10	Colin Osborne

Euro Champs 2010, Dinslaken, Germany:

Round	Result	Opponent
1	6-2	Gary Anderson
2	10-6	Barrie Bates
Qtr	6-10	Terry Jenkins

UK Open 2012, Bolton, England:

Round	Result	Opponent
3	9-7	Alan Tabern
4	9-7	Mark Hylton
5	9-8	Joe Cullen
Qtr	6-10	Denis Ovens

Acknowledgements

Thank you to the following contributors:

Fr. Julian Hollywell SCP

Vicar of Saint Werburgh, Spondon

David Kirby

Author of *The Definitive Darts Coaching Manual* and *Darting Essays – A Coaching Critique*

Ian Gutteridge

Secretary of the Central England Darts League

Wal Capell

Secretary of the Leicester Friday Darts League (previously known as the Leicester Trades Darts League)

The *Leicester Mercury*

For their kind permission to allow the reproduction of Jamie's photos from the *Leicester Mercury* newspaper

Darren Wren

Darts player

Gaz Lynam (Team Jabba)

Photographer